Tell Me the Tr

Bob,

(for our friendship
& for justice,

In solidarity,

Struan

Stuart Rees

Tell Me the Truth About War

GINNINDERRA PRESS

Acknowledgements

Half of the poems in this anthology have not been published before. The remainder have had an earlier public airing in the journals *Southerly, Quadrant, Australian Socialist, Peace Writes* and *Australian Social Work.*

In addition to my insightful and ever patient reader and critic Ragnhild, other members of my family and several very close friends, significant mentors in my poetry have been the late Henry Maas and the poets Robert Pinsky, Vivian Smith and Noel Rowe. As befits creative artists whose focus is a common humanity, they are probably unaware of their influence but I am grateful to them.

First published in this form 2004 by
GINNINDERRA PRESS
PO Box 53 Charnwood ACT 2615 Australia
www.ginninderrapress.com.au

Printed by Pirion Digital, Fyshwick, ACT

Contents

for

Isabella, Holly & Freya

Painting Portraits

Women In Bombay Traffic

A starting gun moves streams
on foot, on carts, over refuse
in honking taxis and in desperation.
The entrants blend with bullocks,
with lean peasants and limbless lepers
nudging, thrusting and loping
in this no-choice contest
to maintain the surging first lap
of a continent's endless congested marathon.

Not lost in a crowd
the women have some secret.
Elegant, supple and smooth
these daubed mothers and daughters
are distinct even if veiled.
Sidestepping the hawkers, buses and beggars
they control their space
with practised intuition
beyond the ken of any coach.

Their motion is born from gender
and a belief
that if they make good time here
they'll compete in other races.
Poverty's struggle is their training ground,
their colourful pacemaking
is derived from a certainty
that there is no alternative
but to keep running.

The Water Buffalo

In times of confrontation
when humility's a feat,
to kill is seen as freedom,
to serve is labelled weak,
we hear the sounds of protest
of rights and rights at length,
how strange to call this animal
of stamina and strength.

Some topped with brass, some painted,
some broken, some not grown,
there are curled and straight and nobbly
yet the faces are forlorn
and neck nobs set the hinges
for worn-out castes and carts
whose shafts have framed the rib cage
which burdens cannot mask.

It must be cheap to run them
on water, love and greens;
yoked to the orient's wagons
they need no gasoline.
Serene in all their plodding,
predictable if slow,
companions to the poorest,
the water buffalo.

Jasmin

Armed with loud gestures
we believed we could share our thoughts
with her bounce
and lessen her frustration.

Visions of shrubs, tropical
colours and perfumes
were not disappointed
in the brown-eyed openness
of playful touching and mouthing
which masked the silent tombs.

Where the surf sight matched its lack of sound
her special world seemed not to matter
and her moustachioed, mild-mannered Dad
reassured anxious neighbours
that everything was normal and if it was not
she would be in danger
of appearing different.

Etiquette-conscious adults smiled back
at the interruptions
to their wish not to be interrupted.
Her buoyancy on her bicycle
made instantly forgotten
her getting her own way needs
for something more than attention.

A kookaburra's chattering signalled the start
of each morning's guessing
at the dark-plaited wishes
of the light-humoured lassie
who triggered notions
of what we thought we heard
or what we wanted to say.

Twyla Tharp

Difficulties in painting electricity
or describing a gardenia's perfume
are illustrated by those

for whom startling bodies
and balance of lines in rhythm comments
would be as predictable as family snaps
which make one holiday look like another.

A lampooning
of the gym shoes craze for aerobics
and a disrespect for lifting or being lifted
begins with a climax
when tradition demands a gradualness
to help the audience prepare

for break, boxing, karate
or classic fused
into bolero crescendos
which give too much to absorb
and have made them screamed-after heroes and heroines.

An athleticism
from scarlet knickers
and blacks and whites in lots of stripes,
called avante garde even in New York,
strikes in pantaloons and skirts
worn to warn of voltage
barely disguised in falls and feints.

In centre front and stage back,
clarity comes from confusion,
simplicity from a chorus of eleven solos
which swirl from mists
to prove the posters' claims
and catch new converts
in the admirers' dilemma
of the performers' brilliance
being matched only
by the stickiness of their perspiration.

On Receiving Michael Dransfield

Frankness becomes
a modest means of revelation
beside Michael's disarming
inside-outs
unmasking outside-ins
which peel and flash
a razor sympathetic injected
with truths scarcely known
in the foggy distance
where transparency's opaque,
spontaneity is felt as fantasy,
risk-taking is wrapped in comprehensive insurance
and secret coupling
rouses no more
than the excitement of politeness
at a Sunday school picnic.

(On the poems of Michael Dransfield, who died in 1973 aged twenty-five)

The Busker

Thousands of hurrying faces
absorbed by tension and time
are looking congested up tunnels
and feeling restricted by grime.

To those who seem deaf from the gazing
through migraines and headline news,
he offers his J.S. Bach healing
for contesting the morning's queues.

Like bullfrogs on lily pads staring
without the calm of the ponds,
only some can heed the prescription
strumming pause, un-listen, come on,

I don't mind your non-contributions
the elegant fingers exclaim,
an echo of treble clef features,
the solvents for spasms and pain.

Laid-back is this tousle-haired busker
whose taut strings can just keep ajar
his no-charge, no-side-effect treatment
to lessen the subway catarrh.

Pilgrimage

A journey's beginning
in the sepia of a childhood denied
in service to adults
preparing for wars

had bred pursed lips
and a burning
for a migrant's heritage

untouched by fear
but inwardly ruled by rules
of a world with little to laugh about.
So emotion showed in fashion

and a fascination with steering
a highway of relationships
with the sap of old convictions.

Her smouldering certainty
a blackened trunk
still erect in the forest,
remained to dress the mourners

and hear the silence of scarlet roses
draping the sobbing of the young woman
whose child she never was,
whose daughter she had always been.

(Tribute to Anna Goller)

Suburban Symphony

Hobbled by lawn mowing
and bankcard arrears,
greying mothers with matching partners
are checking tickets as though pleasure
comes from duty not elation.

Into the town hall
musicians humping black cases
are accompanied by red-brick burghers
pondering a programme
of romantic melodies
with dramatic conclusions.

Through a festive first overture
sombre expressions
are funeral tuned
and conversion to spirit
seems a million to one chance.

For two hours it feels as though a strip show
would pass unnoticed,
yet finally a fifth of Tchaikovsky
lifts even the candidates for old people's homes:
horn seduction lulls them into their first movement,
bassoon grace carries them through a second
and at evening's end
a timpani finale
has stirred a climax
in the composition of their lives.

The Welder

Could have healed Ulster
or joined the Christians to the Shiites
with the same commitment he uses
to peer up the rusty rectum
of my station wagon

while in ungoggled pauses
he explains his forging
of Italian connections
to no-free-lunch principles
and hears complaints
of other casualties

then returns his gun and gaze
to white metal cooling to red
his oxyacetylene sign
to add a two-point-two offering
to seal a kinship lesson
now burned into a repaired muffler
and my recall of welding
in unexpected places.

This Painter in Public

Knows the films
which cinema-goers
savour and recall
like photographs of scenery
and families cherished for smiles
which they thought were their best.

He chooses a blend
of sky, leaves and grass
which they can call their own,
these amateurs wanting technique
yet watching a philosophy
that tones precede colour,
content comes from composure
of easel ease and smudgy palate
from which he brushes greens and browns,
blurs them as a background
for a light and shade second coat
which sharpens bricks into arches
over streams of reflections
exposed by a zigzag touch
which deepens the landscape
as contrasts spark life from indifference.

Toddlers at the Guggenheim

Once in a lifetime
at the Guggenheim
where lines are labelled mandolin
cubes are exposed by spotlights
and planes become accordion,
the gallery-goers shuffle
solemn as pallbearers
or ashamed to admit
they do not understand

while into those space wide-eyed
oblivious of whispers
career two joyful toddlers
laughing at the lights
grinning at a canvas of crotches
and stabbing 'look daddy' fingers
at each piece of dreaming.

They have disturbed a uniform
who had been lulled
by adults' obedience
and is now cued to command
'keep back from here'
but today's rebels
are with the impressionists:
in circles of their own choosing
they are imitating no one
not even themselves.

The Bank Teller

As optimistic as the signs
'please ask us for a loan'
she stands and gives
'can I help you' invitations,
her slants of sun
through autumn's reds and golds
dissecting glum glances
from the withdrawal queues
and from stooped messengers
who are emptying their bags
and counting their cash.

She humours migrant students
who are new to these rituals
and embarrassed academics
who have forgotten their pin numbers
until it is my turn to berth
like a ship docking slowly
tied up and dry in the throat
yet ready to announce:
the other tellers are the cast,
the solo sign says on your breast
you are too precious for this zoo
your smile has moved adrenalin
and surely prompts the vaults to sing.

Rudolph

Your confidence
that you were a great dancer
left little time to fathom
the intrigue in your lips,
the taut or supple music
from your limbs.

In your escapee partnership
with a prima ballerina,
whether in posters
or on a stage,
I imagined your fitness
would last forever.

Instead tonight's news
shows your body ravaged
in a final performance
so I weep for the spirit
which leapt across the world
and has succumbed too early
to the force for which you danced,
to life itself.

(On the death in January 1993 of Rudolph Nureyev; the end of his
partnership with Margot Fonteyn)

Vincent in Victoria

Broad brush strokes
of peasant planters
and potato pickers
are explained in recordings
for silent shufflers
and whispering couples
who have recognised a yellow chair,
a contented postman
and a man in despair

whose sanity
lay in bold gold fields
and soft blue vineyards
reproduced in puzzles and posters,
in papers for wrapping books,
catalogues and shirts

which makes me wonder
if he would have painted a souvenir ship
and if asked to describe his work
what he would say.

The Veteran

Fifty years on in Falaise,
'the gap' and the carnage
are shown in shop windows:
'D-day before and after'
and in the medals
of the blazered in the town square,
a veteran thought full
and grateful to explain
'I was in armoured and only nineteen.'

Silence prompts his wife
tear full, he comes every year,
one day to see the crosses,
to honour the thousands
and a brother whose early summer
was also in Normandy,
who knew no other winters
who shared no other journeys
and did not come back

The Goddess Is Dancing

On a day drummed weary by the news
I slow at lights, expecting nothing,
though a muddy wagon
suggests a chemistry of difference

which is confirmed by a smile
from a driver
whose lips-parted-body-lithe profile
also poses questions;
then taut as her toddler's harness,
still as an azalea
after shimmering in a breeze,
she stares ahead and moves away.

Here was jasmin among carbon,
colour in a chorus
so I am sad to leave her secret,
but a disappearing bumper sticker
solves the mystery,
rescues my day
and forever brands her message in my mind,

'The Goddess Is Dancing'.

Phillipino Maids

Solid on a Sunday
of dressing and touching,
thousands of faces
disguise their separation
by smiling
brown-eyed togetherness.

Conversations cover pavements,
newspapers are tablecloths
and diners are squatting
to share rice and noodles
while savouring snaps
as records
of the signs of this trade.

Through pages from home
today's wind
blows love and nostalgia,
the private news
read in a public place
where tourists sidestep maids
who are guarding their day-off oases,
so far from home,
so near to the below-stairs-days
of another century,
starring other bosses
in another place.

The Squire of Bega

Around a fish and friendship table
my Guinness-spirit mate
ignores his limbs
and sprays the meal with fearful officials,
the limits of electronics
and a history of protests
about the blindness of the bottom line.

His courage is as refreshing
as rains sweeping the southern coast,
his fingers prime glasses
then conjure from the grand
a fistful of Chopin
followed by more indignation
tuned with wrath and laughter
as engaging as his sylph-like wife,
as mellowing as the late-night dram
which complements
the evening's conversation
and the sedative quality of his cat.

Ros of Cessnock

A creamy wattle of a woman
is working
to the chatter of her walkman
and the music of her secateurs.

The pruning season is smiling
on a face browned by land
and on a voice made gravel
by coke and nicotine
which fire these
'keep moving' mottoes:

mother all the children,
treat misfortunes
as parking tickets or speeding fines,
curse them
but not for long enough
to interrupt the vineyard rhythms,
giving life by cutting the dead,
finding stamina for tying the shoots
and joy for inhaling the harvest,

seldom as an achievement
but usually as a time
to re-gather wits, car and kids,
to chastise lazy sons
before switching into the gear
for renewing cheerfulness
in the practice
of your life's hard lessons.

An Academic Mate

In black anorak and yellow car
you drove few miles but travelled far
with theorists, films and poets' looks
for ideas, humour, thoughts and books.
In selfish managerial age
you showed so many unfashionable traits,
rejecting goals of pomp and wealth
you wrote instead the *States of Health*.

Irreverent, funny in style and deed
with taste for gossip and office intrigue
smiling with questions from God knows where,
you fished them in meetings out of the air
and gave to students strength with wings:
flying minus material things,
in room of plants and books askew
references, papers, patience, you
who nurtured youngsters outside, waiting
suggesting 'never be ingratiating,
avoid the shallow, sow the seed
of knowledge gained by read, read, read'.

And now you've gone and won't come back
or perhaps you're lost in the Fisher Stack
with other dead thinkers of creative mind
for underdogs of humankind.
Whatever the reason, there's a hole for us
that you went away without any fuss
ne'er wanting a tribute to be unfurled
we never could enter your private world
of hopes or doubts, love or affection,
yet you gave to others inspiring direction
to write, to think and question 'the factual',
to show the way of the intellectual
searching, unmasking year by year,
thank you, my friend, for your generous career.

Death of a Princess

Brutal played her fragile form
until the last oxygen
was squeezed from the slimlines
amid the mangled metal,
no subject for more pictures
so the paparazzi fled
and the waking felt betrayed
by the numbness of the last act
of their romance with a princess
whose normality they recognised
in acceptance after rejection,
in small victories over depression,
each a reason for signing a book of disdain
for the sentiments of the stoics
as feeling as a flag unfurled
and four days late with their condolences,
so the open-necked
pointed the path of their own identity
which collared protocols advised
would show the cardboard of tradition
but the tabloid men announced
the beauty of imperfection
was the cause of the people's grief,
her going of insufficient purpose
unless new prophets would be heard
in these queues of the dispossessed.

Summer Snap

A question mark is crouching
almost naked on the beach,
the curving line is certain
but the answer's out of reach
to ripples on the water,
to footsteps in the sand
to a mother with her camera
or the pebble in your hand
which contains an ancient secret
like a scout without a map,
the sources of the planets
or the sunshine on your back.

The answer to the question
is as beauty in a pearl,
a heron on a foreshore,
a black bikini girl.

Mopeds of Phnom Penh

If you can imagine a carnival
of riders three or four to a horse,
one astride, the others side-saddle,
their kids perched at crazy angles
supervised by proud fathers in peak caps
and sleek young women loving the breeze
as hundreds of coloured stallions
charge like an undisciplined cavalry
through clouds of cannon smoke,

you have forgotten any semblance of a highway code
but you have seen the mopeds of Phnom Penh

The Beggars of Angkor Wat

With microchip precision
and the confidence of divine right
the riches of these ancient kingdoms
were enshrined in towers and temples
and carved in stone tapestries
of warriors with escorts
of monkeys and elephants
and trumpeters announcing
the majesty of athletes
marching to battle,
blessed by Hindu gods
and given courage
by the certainty of karma.

With all the ingenuity
of human neglect
the glory has disappeared,
weapons are now buried,
the jungle has eaten the detail
and around every corner
like a monument to modernity
the limbless squat pleading
their caps mostly empty
the majesty of their bodies crumbling,
not over centuries but before our eyes.

Candide, Philosophy of Optimism

Dr Pangloss has a recipe
for optimism which defies
shipwrecks, executions and floggings
even if fighting for causes
and the effect of being
with Jesuits or against them
in the battle of all persuasions
for churches in countries
where international law is observed
if all the citizens of besieged towns
have been slaughtered
and women are whoring
to pay the rent
for harbour houses where fidelity
is relative to the pox
which leaves you lucky to lose only one ear
and hope lives on if you keep one limb.

Yet Eldorado stays as the dream
in a story of love in port and pore
where friendship survives to show
wisdom in losing thrones
and deciding to be kings no more
by dropping the trappings
and letting your garden grow
in the best of all possible worlds.

Unique Humanitarian

(for Gordon Rodley)

In slides of the moon's beams
from archaeological sites
and through a telescope erected
at the rear of a Camperdown flat,
he built disrespect for boundaries
but joy in friendships forged
in reflections
on the stamina of Simpson's donkey,
the persistence of Bruce's spider
and the courage of them both.

A writer of well argued tracts,
a scientist sceptical of facts,
he saw life's truths in groves of pine
and top spin backhands down the line,
his game of life devoid of rorts
but peppered with his peaceful thoughts
which tapped the strength of silence born
like poets waiting for the dawn
to paint ideals in diverse places,
to conjure smiles in sombre faces
he pricked ol' class pomposity
with selfless generosity,
tho' tumours got him in the end,
it was my prize to have this friend.

Corroboree 2000

A man of gentleness
asked us to speak quietly to those who
question revision of a history
whose centrepiece was cast aside
when Mabo overturned the myths of emptiness,
dispossession showed its jagged edges,
stolen generations started to come home
and a rainbow of young voices sang
that no one could steal the future.

Once disguised by the best of intentions,
broken families and deaths in custody
showed first people being last
but today's walkers for reconciliation
have been confirmed by the silent silver
writing its fluffy white on parchment blue
by diving in lines and circles
to spell 'sorry' above the bridge
and in the freedom of the sky.

Nelson in September

The build-up was like waiting for a bride
to give the cue to stand, to turn and gaze
at this handsome suitor armed with selfless deeds,
a groom who is marrying
the shirt he's asked to wear
in stripes of Africa's opposing team,
so Gandhi-like he teaches you and me
to shower with love each polar enemy.

A sonnet is too short to catch this man
of sunlight on the global seas of grey
where poverty condemns and disempowers
the millions who would lift and be inspired
by being here to breathe, to learn to see
this beacon light for all humanity.

The Skinks

These guardians of the garden
have found a way to live,
they worship sun on sandstone rocks
and find their homes on country blocks,
they hide within the wand'ring jew
to watch the giants stumble through.

These spritely imps whose arms are legs
know where nutrition lies,
their darting lives are not far fetched
'cos tongues are brains and always stretched
to taste and teach them what to keep,
to always turn the other cheek.

They're long and short but always slim
extended groups of kith and kin
whose early warning system shows
the wisdom of their decoy doze:
when seeming ready for a fight,
they lose their tails in flight and fright.

Once said to be for medicine,
the therapy is watching them
and calculating debts we owe
to constant creatures on the go,
so if this world is wise and thinks,
'twould find a better name than skinks.

Goodbye Harry

Harry leaving the stage
requires a poem for a Pickwick
who could sing like Caruso
and wink as a larrikin
before the altar of his songs of praise
and in Seagoon falsettoes
ensure that the unplanned
found the spot where listeners wanted to be.

Superlatives are flowing
for a Bumble
whose pantomime circumference
around Britain and Broadway
showed the present as farce
and promised
that pontificators would be heard
but never taken seriously
as long as his giggling at our worries
was laced with Welsh-valley loveliness.

He will not hear these analogies
but the thought of this tenor
singing at his own funeral
with frangipani fragrance
is producing a tribute
which he would goon over with his mates
along with the image of a swell
surging with love and applause.

He will not be emulated
unless we expand our girth and repertoire,
mouth to a tape of his antics,
revere the irreverent
and so recall a performer
nurtured by a faith so great
that it freed him
from the strain of keeping up appearances.

Five verses is not enough
for the Goon who gave life
to so many
'did you hear that one?' conversations
among friends learning their own buffoonery
by trying to capture highs
which he reached
but which others could only try to imitate.

At least we can be grateful
for this life-enhancer
and reflect on the epitaph
that he suffered fools gladly
because he was happy to be one of them.

(marking the life of singer, Goon and actor Harry Secombe, who died
on 12th April 2001)

Swiss Misses of Geneva

As ordered as the city gardens,
as distinct as their white on red flag,
as apparently unassailable
as the castle of Baron M. de Rothschild,
and as confident as the fountain of Geneve
which sprays the villas where Lord Byron stayed
and shore lines where young Shelley lived,
in fitted leather and tight light blue
the young Swiss misses,
decorated by carefree but careful hair
above brown tans and dark stockings,
noses slightly airborne
and oblivious of anyone making notes about them,
are sauntering the cobbles.

As civil as you would expect
from a parade of handsome buildings
housing all the means of intervention to secure our freedoms –
international labour to world trade
to Europe's seat for the UN
to the Palais Wilson – described
in a mistaken, un-Swiss brochure
as the headquarters 'of the High Comision of the Human Hights' –
the young Swiss misses
pause with fashionable bags,
sip coffee, wave cigarettes
and ever so slightly fondle their jewellery
before moving like catwalk models
to their next engagement.

As comfortable as the coiffured slopes,
some as spectacular
as views of the Mont Blanc massif
and all as interesting as the migrating birds
who motel in the reed beds,
the young Swiss misses
with their suntans and stockings
in up-to-date shoes
to complement up-the-thigh skirts
do not immediately convey
a capacity for sex or intrigue
though Josephine de Beauharnais,
the first wife of Napoleon Bonaparte,
lived by the water beyond the cobbles,
so something must be going on.

Boats On the Beach

In full sail, portly ladies stroll.
Measured, dimpled, straw-hatted,
thickened by motherhood, slowed by caring
they display the resolution
of well maintained tugs in high seas.
The shape of their confidence prompts attention
but a different reaction
follows a proud and erect mast
on a craft silking with slender rigging
across the sand.

Assessed by spectators
she moves like a state-of-the-art yacht
whose scanty decorations
exaggerate her secrets,
perhaps a balanced bow or keel,
or even navigation instruments,
so who cares whether she is brainless or a genius,
no one knew what Mona Lisa was thinking
yet millions still queue
to see a picture they will never forget.

Poetry Is My Camera

'Strange,' said the young Indian women
in the courtyards of the orphans' homes,
'you come without a camera.
Most visitors want to take pictures
of children and traffic through crowded slums.
Without a record to take home,
how will you know the sights and smells,
the faces and the places,
how will you recall
our answers to your questions?'

Without the clutter of a shutter
or a fiddling with a lens,
consciousness can live in pencilled thoughts
and glimmer-of-ideas-scribblings
marinated in images of –
nostalgia for the loved long gone,
an outrageous injustice
which gallops into view
as suddenly as the sky at night –
each needing to be developed
in black or white or colour,
perhaps explained but never enlarged.

Whatever its label or size,
the camera is as obvious as a ringed nose
and can be as intrusive as a teacher
who is reluctant to allow her pupils
to tick over at the speed of a convoy,
or parents who want prodigies
to grow by avoiding their past mistakes.
It can be observed
even if the photographer
is as subtle as a choreographer
who outlines form but seldom steps.

My means of carrying the mind's eye
into the orifices of life,
provides the chance to feel a high
from treasures discovered,
or from healing by unmasking lows,
yet to claim no weight in carrying
this equipment is as illusory
as to say there is no discipline
in entering the darkroom
to ponder plays on words
or to read the rhythms
from the latest rolls of film.

Joy comes in knowing
that a topic for a title will emerge
without the aid of Kodak, Konika or Canon
and in a day of taking pictures
no one may suspect my trade or intention.
I am free without a case or leather strap
and no protruding paraphernalia,
not even the disposables
held by clickers who hope
that something permanent will be born
from little boxes thrown away
once the holiday has ended
the wedding party has sobered up
and the marriage has been consummated.

Each prospect of creating pictures
without placing a notepad on a tripod –
to encourage ideas to be still,
to ensure they stay in focus –
is like driving through a city without fumes
with every light turned green,
like floating in turquoise then landing yoga-like,
uncoiled upon a white sand shore
washed, roused and ready
to tilt the kaleidoscope
whatever the attitude of the clouds,
the demeanour of passers-by
or the weather in their eyes.

In lights of shade at varying speeds
a photographer's subjects
can be zoomed in and out,
placed and poised at different angles
then printed for the pleasure
of those who enjoy looking at themselves,
yet to capture moments
in snapshots worth sharing,
my camera must saunter the shadows
to reach beyond the immediate
for lines which no one might have expected
and just by looking
may never have seen.

Meeting The Dalai Lama

Nurtured by Buddhism and mountains,
with homilies honed by the romance
of a refugee
who courts enemies as friends,
he teaches that hearts
find solutions to conflicts by drawing breath
in silence-reducing emotions
to massage minds and connect
to conditions for being humane.

For tensions religious and politics
he carries prescriptions
of compassion and humour,
age-old sedatives and vitamins
for living with life's contradictions –
violence with passive resistance,
possessions valued yet worthless –
to realise a life blood from spiritual harvests.

He is a sports occasion under lights,
moonlight down a coast across a bay,
an awakening for each morning
happy as a kookaburra laughing,
he is my wife hearing others' sorrows
finding salves for strains and wounds,
he is balance beneath an orange haze,
a loose fit of yellow and burgundy,
armchaired between purple and white flowers.

Refugee Story

Work hard seven days a week
for seven years and then
feel rice mixed with tomatoes
for another seven years
impossible life, must leave
but how, confide in mother
so gold the only answer
she says, pay to get out,
gold to bribe policemen
keep quiet about leaving
travel down from highlands
to lowlands coast for boats,
lucky as I fit young man
not scared and don't care if I die,
but sea not blowing too much
boat four days to Malaysia
four months in refugee camp
lucky again immigration
interview for Australia
not know where that is
but no more bribes needed,
goodbye to family,
goodbye to controls,
sorry for family
not sorry for controls,
out to airport and flight
to new country with no luggage
and no word of language
not even 'yes' or 'no',

lucky again, up comes job
with Ford company
soon wages so chicken comes with rice
later married with Vietnam wife
then two real Aussie sons,
to day for refugees
escape more difficult,
can't explain it but perhaps
just fit and young and lucky.

Street Players of Rome

Between pizzeria and blue iced gelato
a violinist and a guitarist
struggle for happiness,
a boy on an accordion
and his cymbal-shaking mother
show hints of rhythm
but no one has asked them to play.

Before the ovens of the Coliseum,
black, smiling and perspiring
sun glass sellers from Senegal
have laid out their Gucci Valentino imitations
for sales to send home
when the heat subside
and the tourists have flown away.

Close to yet far removed from
Michelangelo's mercy for the crucified,
lasagne, tortellini and spaghetti suppers
are indifferent
to the hangdog looks and upturned palms
of pleading women
whose fragile business lies
where homelessness looks permanent,
where poverty will be the matinee of another day.

The Jam Man of Huskisson

From yellowed pages of a last century
of great grandmother recorded recipes
dependent on home-grown essentials
minus any conception of additives,
he preserves the palates of the past
by converting her pencilled wisdom
into chutneys, sauces, marmalades and jams.

His only advertising
is a street side sign for screw-tops
to secure mulberries, guavas and cumquats
in the mixtures of a home-grown geneticist
searching for strains of sweetness and vigour
by feeding sugar to vegetables and spices to fruit
from plants we seldom thought we could eat.

On his veranda he peels and chops.
On an elderly gas stove he wheezes
into a platoon-sized saucepan
whose froth settles as he stirs.
In an outhouse the labelled are readied
for the rusty ringing of lip smackers
who love the choices and the flavours
from this antidote for the supermarket,
this midwife of a forgotten craft,
the country town man with an age-old gift for jam.

Man in the Linen Suit

Dressed to address,
bespectacled, silvered, Pickwickian
and plump with ideas
which he casts like ripe apples,
to be picked and savoured
or, like jacaranda blossoms,
to be scuffed, sniffed and admired.

As adamant as a force-eight gale,
as persistent as an ass,
the appearance of a grand inquisitor
intent on sentencing his opponents
is belied by a belly of thesaurus proportions,
a source of protest as arguments tire
and warm presence as the brandy beckons.

A mixture of class frustrations,
aristocratic airs, Liverpudlian nous
and Irish disdain for the Protestant ethic,
soccer scores show his tribal loyalties,
and as memorable as the lines of his classic cars,
a beautiful woman rounds his sharp edges.
Yet it is the Catholic-coloured testaments
which make his convictions
as consistent as his prayers,
as weather beaten and durable
as the linen suit
which he wears for all occasions.

The Palestinian Representative

His chapter titles include
expulsion and separation,
destruction on lands lost
and on another continent
a rebuilding of hopes of being heard
by sceptics and opponents
who have not recognised the nurture
derived from his conviction
'as long as we exist we shall win'.

He is a warrior who can laugh
at the stereo of desert nomads
unfamiliar with the suits of false claims
and the veneer of small talk.
His survival is the dignity of existence,
assertion is the signal of optimism,
his warmth has been insulated
by the attrition of suspicion,
so his trusted conversations
are with press releases,
Aminah, his children and his books.

Intense-eyed focus
to sustain this freedom
looks like sandhill running
with history and Israeli tanks
strapped to his back, a weight he accepts
as preparation for the day
when courage forged by one-way choice
sees the killing end, the refugees return
and in leafy Narrabundah
his office become an embassy
where his smile will reappear
on the face of an ambassador.

Socialist with a Human Face

From appearances in tributes
he is a weather-hardened bosun
whose books were his compass,
whose articles of resistance
created charts for others to follow.

His marching understanding
with those who enjoyed
the devil in his humour,
forged friendships
as nurturing as his romance with Shelley.

As unencumbered by possessions
as wild geese flying south for winter,
he inspired those who watched
by staying airborne
towards only one destination.

He found the winds to blow
over the sludge of hypocrisy,
his words flowed unstoppable
towards ideals that anyone might ride
the motion from his waves.

He was against the violence of conquerors,
he saw as no better than spivs
those who posed in politics
or sold phoney products
even from judges' benches.

He was for the disadvantaged,
the hair shirts of conscience
and the stifled
who needed his replies
as evidence of their innocence.

Never an optional extra,
his radicalism was the bloodstream,
his self mockery an abiding badge
even for the crutches
of his final years.

(Tribute to journalist Paul Foot, 1937–2004)

Revealing Occasions

Seventeenth of May

Early morning's rising mists
sweep roads of homes
and lanes of birch where students
already decorated and bugle blowing
wake the town.

Inside a dress rehearsal
of girls scarlet in skirts,
blonde women embroidered into linens
and lace treasured from earlier celebrations,
the men supple in blue
yet bold in starched white, their shirts
ready to go.

Outside an excited hum
of listening to martial music
waltz-like in its gaiety of skipping children
ushered into rows
fluttering flags of blood red on blue
and following pied-piper-like
between the trees.

This unison
of cenotaph respect and wedding festival
can spread the balm and set the course
for all the other days   so
mothers thrill to have their children home
and every generation needs
not even Grieg
to feel at peace
in crashing chords
certain as Hardanger, Geiranger
and fjord-deep.

Burning grey in the midday heat
smoke from Slottsfjell's cannon
parades its own salute
to birthdays in flash green
covering silver traces of braid
while the brass men laughing,
drain their tubas
and seek their partners.

Families saunter home
to garden tables laid
for more reunions
climaxed by more hugging
and emotions laced
with fresh aroma
of black coffee.

Still in their pleasure,
uncluttered by thoughts of work or war,
grandparents, nut-brown from the fresh air
of experience,
recall the same but novel pictures
while the children
freed from dancing and marching,
white smocks smeared,
buttons and hands unclasped at last,
queue for the cake.

(Refers to the annual celebrations of Norway's national day)

Ice Cream

At whose suggestion we can't be sure
but it seemed the only thing to do
at the time.

The sweating tar of an off-beat road
meandered past a pavement picture gallery
of blocks, hearts and cones,
all painted. Some with faces
and even an el-cheapo version
called a paddle pop
which children like.

The novelty of possessing something unique
which also smacked of forbidden fruit
and was not a three hundred and thirty third print
was irresistible and
accompanied by the bonus
of where they were and who they were with.
So, their bargain buys signalled
the indulgence of teenage experiment
and their laughter
tumbled along the melting way.

They strolled and licked,
framed by the flop of the surf
on a gentle day,
the one encased in chocolate
the other stuffed with peaches
preserved by the intimacy
of cold cream.

It will be difficult
to re live this piece of high summer
though the suggestion to freeze the imagery in verse
is one a way of recalling tastes, temperatures
and the fine art prospect
of doing it
all over again.

On Hearing of a Serious Injury

Blood was running from the flame tree
spilling vitality against a darkening sky
when the telephone rang its forbidding news.

Serious adjectives
were the monotone in a breezeless night
conveying the horrors
of multiple fractures, fifty-fifty chances, brain damage
and instructions to 'expect the worst',
'call again tomorrow'.

Occasions of death's imminence
will always be unrehearsed.
My feelings were caught off guard,
present but shapeless,
the colour of grey gums without rain,
a mixture of stillness and odourless disbelief
interrupted by pit of the stomach spasms
from sudden pictures of sadness that might have been smiles
clouded by regretful questions
unspoken and unknown to the distant voice of the close relative
who impressed me as a model of control
in her duty of details
when the response from the other end
could have been a justified cry in the dark.

And out of my telephone window
the trunks of the trees
are framed massive above multiple life support systems
guaranteeing a hundred new springs
withering one day perhaps
yet never to be cruelly snuffed out.

Spill-over in a Park

Above clipped grass stands a witness
to a city's litter-be-in-it intentions.
This one's contents had grown
into a rickety castle
which balanced, then tumbled and spread.

As a sentinel for the other refugees
with whom it has come to rest,
a blue thong
befriends burger remains and striped straws
linked with Taurina Spas, Fantas and Colas
which prop up full-fat milkers
and a skimmed variety
for the low cholesterols.

Brown bottles sleep
empty on their sides
nudging their neighbours
the king-size filters and smooths
who still gleam reminders
of the ad men's mastery
of machismo and romance.

All this junk lies gazing
at monuments to millionaires
and their management of impressions
of sunshine families furnished
like the foyer of an ample hotel
where the manicured and perfumed
lounge in leather as though
garbage plays no part in their lives.

Down the road the spilt bin testifies
to inhalers, swiggers and fantasisers
who may not smell an entrance hall
of disinfected concrete
but to whom I am grateful
for leaving this contrast
and the seagulls' breakfast.

Kitty's Beach

There is no telephone beneath the crystal
where the stingray ponders
and some striped mechanics
inspect the barnacles.

On virgin sand
a marsh fly imposes charges
on trespassers
who had towelled their claim

while casual supervisors
the dipping rising dolphins
want nothing for local calls.

In suspension
with undemanding companions
I am watching
a mugger feller lurking

in a submerged garden
of silvery self space disconnected
from the drizzle of the southerly change.

Circling

Playful silver in the blue high
silence in sunlight
and flickers of angles
of outstretched necks and dipping wings

makes these surfers of the thermals
the superior species
stars of their own sensation
needing the cushions of currents
and the catch of a slipstream occasion
to seem radio-controlled

for the time is theirs
and so is the space of their graceful
courtship by circling.

Tinnsjoen from Sandviken

A clean river
empties into a mirror
and in the mountains
dignity answers back.

On the shore
the still pines stand
and an old rowboat
promises a day beneath cotton fluffs.

In early summer
large birches are vikings
and busybody wagtails
play at trolls to ensure

the fjord sides descend
with the permanence of picture postcards
while all around
has a fresh trout taste
and the air
lays tang on the cheeks.

Cabin at Myklebostad

From the windows of this distant cabin
silhouettes of all the world's beauties
are flirting with the mountain shadows,
they are stretching on the mossy foreshore
preparing to dance across the waters
towards the curtains of evening
certain to receive applause
from all who have climbed to learn
that fantasies can be realised
when framed by a majesty
which dwarfs all the world's small ideas.

Lower Murray

On the river's final lap
South-westers give whitecaps
to the brown water,
and terns,
all angles and nosedives
are enjoying their last playground
before the southern ocean.

Among the reed beds,
disdainful of the moan
of an overloaded outboard,
unhurried swans
are black with majesty
while dusky moorhens
are sprinting the waves.

Beyond the mouth, mayhem
but here, hovering before gusts,
descending in their wake,
landing composed
then floating away,
the one-eyed pelican
is the keeper of humanity.

Bottlebrush Tree

Outside my cabin,
swollen with pollen
she stands and sways,
her scarlet brushes
an invitation
to a hubbub of bees

who are sucking with relish and panic
as though this is the last life support system,
this tree of faith and celebration
as exultant as a crowd
who have just heard that their city
has won the Olympic games.

Power Cut

I wanted to fry bacon and eggs
when Andrew Olle was stopped
in mid-flight with a lady
who was talking of a coup in selling
Australian flavoured ice cream in Beijing.

I did not hear that story's end
but felt lost by my inability
to adjust to a morning aborted
by someone else's overload

at which point my neighbour,
also hobbled
by plans with time slots,
complains
that she cannot vacuum her carpet.

Immobilised
by dependence on the expected
and by inexperience of tidal waves
or simple readiness
for the modestly unexpected,

my only response
– it took twenty minutes to get around to that –
was to scribble the missing-my-bacon piece,
hope the radio interviewer recovers
and tomorrow
my neighbour's carpets can be cleaned.

(Reference to the popular ABC radio 2BL compere Andrew Olle)

Black Swans

In red and black livery
two aristocrats of the estuary
shepherd four children
in a heads-down bottoms-up survey
then surface to sail away
certain
in the S-bends of their silhouettes,
confident
that the dignity of their leaving
shows
that it is not always necessary
to know where you are going.

Poetry Workshop

(for Henry Maas)

Here is your chance with handouts,
your own photocopies
and the lingering
of single impressions
to describe things that cannot be said.

Please say how your creations
were sculpted and where
and what turned you on
to pursue inner voices
despite the mystery of how to start.

Everyone can hide their silence
by reading out loud;
and to a wider world
we may even publish
a collection of the loosely bound.

Our newcomers might feel
like non-swimmers on a high board
but I encourage you
not to be discouraged
by thinking of the ultimate dive.

Remember, everything is possible:
you could end with a fine form line
as in the touch of finding time
for repetition in a rhyme
loaded with picture and with pun
conceived by something called pure fun.

Visiting a Poet in Hospital

(for Ann Ptolemy)

Like a firefly resting
on a lily pad
I find you searching
for the freedom of a foal let loose,
finding in hugs of esteem
courage to lessen despair,
smiling with mischievous questions
beneath a brown mass curly
as you must have been
on a first school day
when skies beckoned
and sages would not have predicted
this refuge of bed signs and uniforms
and recall of burger-size morphine shots
to sustain a life of composing
at least one apple a day
to keep the cats in the head at bay,
to protest the next lows
and the permanent highs
and to encourage perhaps
some semblance of sleep.

One Walk Two Lives

Across the harebells, over stiles,
between the cattle and the sheep,
we met two lives.

The first – walking with his dogs –
talking in cavalry twills
and designer-label vowels,
showed how education and investments
could be converted into self-confidence
which he exhaled in asides about the weather,
thirty-five years in Rome, several in Washington
and a couple 'in that house in the hills',
snaps shown as extras to unusual August warmth.

So we scanned fields with unspoken questions,
perhaps a diplomat or actor,
choreographer – such poise –
not a banker – he seemed not to calculate –
a novelist, or did we want him to be one,
a secret service remarkable man
who would always be unsuspected
if others were absorbed in standing
listening and mouthing 'goodbyes',
revealing nothing of themselves
and learning next to nothing about him.

A mile away the second – at first unseen
in a farm of tumbledown indifference
to competition and the earnestness
of others who huffed and puffed through his yards –
seemed rusted to his tractor,
a scarecrow familiar with lost looks.

He clambered down
then stared for ten minutes into sixty years,
beginning with a cast of Irish labourers
who picked potatoes,
moved to beet then south to soft fruit,
horses who worked as friends
then in production pressure disappeared,
each loss sandwiched 'tween seasons and sound barriers
which the grizzled traversed
in sweltering heat and thick dialect,
matching shirt, canvas trousers and rubber boots.

He wiped his brow
with diesel-lacquered knuckles,
no pretensions and few concessions,
as arable changed to animals,
yards accumulated the obsolete,
the Nature Trust mapped him at a junction
where walkers might learn
he had seen many faces by going nowhere,
if you cherished the dales they would nourish you
and none could taste the hills by hurrying.

In the Doghouse

A tavern of raw country plenty
looked over the shore to the sea,
oak walls and full blooded menus
for walkers and locals and we

who sat by a worn wooden table
while blonde maid gave welcome remark,
slim serving in faded blue denims,
she listed the light and the dark.

We pondered, she paused,
we ordered, she smiled,
we were caught by the charm in her voice
and the firmly held breasts
which gave shape to the bar
so we knew we had made the right choice.

Reading Poetry Again

Headaches and restless nights
tightened the tensions
of the deadlines
which answered even the kids'
innocent pocket money requests
with the writer's irritant
'don't waste my time'

and a glimpse at summer's arrival
in the slit up the side
of the willowy girls walking
the colourful streets
has been another diversion
I thought I could not afford.

A sudden waking in a mean motel
at 3.25 a.m.
followed by the same-day bleary insight
that the pale applause for the product
was not worth the lurching fog,
is inscribed by the slow down
space for pondering
some poets' showing
how to pause and how to paint
high ways to live
through breathing a rhythm again.

Viennese Café

Well groomed strudels and spirited tortes
tease strawberry flans and Esterhazy slices
in a daily parade
before the essential ingredients
of the beautifully painted upholders
of another Viennese summer.
Elsewhere in Europe
are perestroika struggles
and North Sea oil disasters

Here the mirrored walls
show bangled wrists
and dangled lobes
in coffee-with-which-pastry dilemmas
and the only disappointment
is the enveloping of subtle perfumes
by the reassuring odour
of street-blown horse manure.

Glasgow Taxi Ride

The planned poverty
rumbled past my paid silence
but the cavernous seat
was filled with riches
as we travelled to Queen Street.

Beneath a pall of cloud
and through the sliding panel
the smoking warmth fired
his let's-blow-our-own-trumpet devotion.

Black tenements' hairy walls
have been waxed white,
the city's industrial crutch facelifted
by facades for flash flats,
the architects have been sentenced
the waters have been flushed to breathe
and waste lands can be gardens
if we blow for long,
it's about time.

His Glasgow pride
shamed the clicking meter
to show a Celtic character
of mateships and memories
and loyalties as long as the Clyde.

Moscow State Circus

On a candy floss day
beneath a big top,
a prospect of legends
has lured hundreds
to savour a communal state
which trained legions of artists
to entertain millions,
some of whom are watching
the high-cheeked Elena
and her sinew-strewn twin
spin as propellers
in thigh-stretched lines
whose climax is the signal
for trapeze-second timing
and highwire juggling,
steel-nerve reminders
of a revolution
which gave gravity to circuses
and is pinning us to our seats,
not graceful yet grateful
to catch breath between
Igors, Olegs and Svetlanas
who carnival our thoughts
with pom-pom illusions
that artistry
may grace our lives
by lighting dull days
with these memories to take home.

Morning Perfection

Pinks and blues are falling into the hills
and crayoning the waters
where bills, gulls and swans
have filled the canvas of the artist
who has given this stillness
to photographers   gazing
with tripods firm and wonders lost,
breathing steam before a startling dawn,
rubbing hands above a sparkling frost.

Lightning Ridge to Walgett

A slightly bendy, mostly straight
occasionally rising road
is bordered by gums and grasses
where emus graze
untroubled by the passing coach
which is navigating
nervous wallabies and confused sheep
while at intervals on taut lines
the highway supervisors,
the confident kookaburras,
sit, composed and watchful,
shunning only the last kilometres
of large grain-silo space
which gives no place to perch
save on a sign saying
'rest at the Coolabah Hotel'.

Lorikeets in the Flame Trees

More casual than highwire acrobats,
more confident than lovers in a trance,
they tiptoe before turning
sideways and upside down
to find nutrition or aphrodisiac
by relishing and ravishing the flowers

and as if their excitement
was insufficient to attract an audience,
they also perform in extravagant costumes,
a green, yellow and orange kaleidoscope
of entertainers on bare twigs
twisting in search of blood-red blooms.

Mornington

Eucalyptus cliffs
descend to seas
where sailors sailed
in search of water to stay alive

and then came painters
to marvel at the light
which filtered the down-under continent
as different but comforting

for the later city 'scapers
searching for sand
but needing nostalgia
for an age which they redesigned
in beach huts squeezed together
like happy crowds fashioned for summer
and fashionable in multicoloured roofs and doors
which now parade the peninsula
and decorate the golden shore.

Huskisson in the Rain

Down a street as uncomplicated
as the free parking,
the town is patrolled
by the growl of old station wagons
and by diesel from four-wheel drives
while holidays in shorts
protest the southerlies
by seeking refuge at the pictures.

By the jetty,
cruise boats
are waiting for dolphin watchers,
oxygen racks for wet suits,
bait shops for the hook, line and sinker men
and bulgers in thongs
for the tavern to open.

'Internationally famous fish and chips'
with oily aromas
offer warm parcels
sprinkled with salt and vinegar
for kids bored with parents
and with tramping wet pavements.

Guarded at one end of sand and sea
by gum tree sentries
and at the other
by Meryl Streep and Clint Eastwood
inserts in an apricot cinema,
the sodden walk in different directions
yet in the same way
as plastic is the fashion for the day.

On a Twenty-hour Journey:
Life From an Aircraft Seat

There is a beautiful woman on the screen
and another sitting beside me,
an air hostess with red lipstick on an old fashioned face
is repeating 'more water?'...'more water?'
followed by a blonde with dark roots
asking 'care for tea?'...'care for tea?'
which distracts a Schumann cello concerto
while sunset sinks through the clouds
as I dip into Raymond Carver
writing with no frills about fishing, old lodgings,
absent children and a forgetful mother
which makes me wander
between a white-shirted Thai steward offering coffee
and my regrets that on this last visit home
I missed the opportunity
to tell my parents how much of great value
they had crammed into their lives,
to find space to hear my father's tales of war at sea,
to drum up the courage to answer my mother's questions
'how long have I got?', 'how do people leave this world?'
just as a violin seductive in the final movement
of Vivaldi's *Winter Concerto* fills the headphones
and completes its own journey by crossing the ice
to another side and for the very last time.

Courtyard in Berry

A fountain flows
over terracotta,
a green tree canopy
protects customers
who are chewing their difficulties in parking
while the sweat of love in prospect is absent,
there being no intense young men
trying to disguise
their interest
in summer's skin-clad young women.

Like dobs of mayonnaise on salad,
white flowers decorate the hedge
which has crept over a fence
to corral tables and tiles,
filter the breeze
and generate the feeling
which books on meditation
can only prescribe:
the deliciousness of being
temporarily cut off from the world.

Much-needed Much-missed

Silent understanding
in time made effortless
by guessing the thoughts of passers-by,
is inhaled at tables
where iced water and salads
accompany our second-hand bookshop buys,
from Kant's metaphysics of morals
to Fred Hoyle's astronomical lessons
and the Picador book of erotic verse.

Silent understanding
of pleasure that a waitress
has invited us to stay all day
is confirmed
in efforts to sketch identity
by realising balance
between ironed-smooth city slickers
and the ulcerated, stockings-down old lady
who pushes her possessions
in a supermarket trolley.

Silent understanding
is a bonus
from this Paradiso on the pavement
whose time
for reading between the lines
has produced a palate for the wine
and a conviction
that when such theatre is relived,
we will know how much we have needed
and how much we have missed.

Seeing and Not Seeing the Spring

Blossoms are licking a sudden warmth,
butterflies are dancing a dervish
and buds are about to explode.

Below a hill of copse
an oxbow meanders
past handfuls of ramblers
who are smearing their nostrils with spring
while back in the nursing home,
with their backs to the windows,
slumpers are slurping their tea.

They seem to know
that winter's grey is becoming blue,
that butterflies are somewhere
and blossoms may be everywhere
but they are mostly motionless
and all are marooned,
conversation has been cancelled
and the biscuits in their saucers
are no substitute
for being unable to breathe the balm
or to see the lazy river.

Orgasms in North Sydney

In the rush to carry cappuccinos
to air-conditioned spaces
office conscripts dash over zebras
stretching towards the mood
to scan emails, shuffle papers,
hear the stored-up calls, read the faxes
in gear which they would not wear
if they could see boats bobbing in the harbour
screened by columns which are alight at night
but contain them today as they move
the boys dark-suited, spiky and tied-up,
the girls short-skirted, brushed and nyloned down,
no one appearing comfortable,
all seeming intent on the foreplay
of this march of economic reason
to sustain electronicus interruptus

which few would die for and daily
takes seven hours to reach any kind of climax
by which time they are pondering the pub,
hailing taxis, disappearing down station steps
ties loosened, stockings not entirely intact
dodging more cars, looking incapable
of participating in any explosion
even if ignited or invited
so they finger their mobiles
to announce they are on their way
for more than another takeaway
to get ready for another day.

Bus Ride to Bethlehem

For twelve shekels passed hand to hand
in a twelve-seater which fumes in the heat
and stops where people wait in rare shade,
we rumble along where that donkey trod
to the town where they brought gifts
to the spot where it all began.

Each stretch is inhaled
by our brown-as-the-desert companion
whose face is lined like the alleyways
on a map of the old city,
whose gaze is a still
of the history in the hills,
who questions 'which religion?'
so that he can locate us
in this Middle East mosaic
of plots and allegiances
lacquered by dust
which covers each checkpoint
and disguises each sect
as though there has been no conflict,
as though the people are one
and the faiths are all the same.

Visiting Assisi

Of all the leaders called a saint
here is one to imitate,
his simple texts are tolled by bells,
an old yet ageless proverb tells
of customs conceived in the east
to love all those considered least,
from bearing wounds endured by others
to treating refugees as brothers,
uncluttered lines devoid of tricks,
a people's third-way politics.

St Francis' sign is strict yet warm,
a jazz conceived for each new dawn
to march in step in tonsured lock
at ease in sandals, tattered smock
hardly the gear for spun TV
yet promise for a century
which might find still a sense of hope
from penance of the knotted rope
to dispossessed-descriptive word
for comfort of a double-edged sword.

Swinging

In eucalyptus shade
above the woodchips of a playground
cooled by north-easterly blusters

– far away from Iranian earthquakes
Christmas road tolls
or the dark intentions of Serb nationalists –

is play in motion as old as memories
as ropes tied to branches
and darings to sway across water
to fall triumphant on muddy banks by village ponds
and feel the seat knot released
until the next time chance
to glide the measure of careless days
as smoothly as a catamaran to shore,
as satisfied as the thirsty on cold beer,
as happy as honeyeaters finding nectar.

The same elation
is etched in the face of a one-year-old
clasping and laughing
through one hundred degrees
of old pleasures reignited
in the unhindered magic
of her swinging.

Summer Siren

Over rippled water
the sound of flapping sails
is broken by an outboard
pulling wetsuits on skis
and children towed in tyres.

Nothing in the day's heat
predicts more than neighbours
in conversation over fences
while a few dog exercisers
– prompted by guilt and pudding –
are plodding with their friends
along the waterfront streets.

The unexpected noise of sudden speed
announces another
'show me yours and I'll show you mine'
which scrèeches into the afternoon
to divide the highs of a holiday
from the wretchedness of assassination.

A dull thud then silence
tells the island
that blind pleasure is a lethal mix
splayed out by clash
of fragile spines and iron stobie
which becomes the site for sirens
wailing for the bonnet and the boys
who will never return to taste
any other excitement
nor quench a thirst for holiday
by sipping beer,
hauling a hull
or wrapping sails.

A Community of Junks

Portly and content
they ride the open sea
and career this harbour
without comment
from bare-footed women
on toe-controlled throttles.

On benches beneath tarpaulins
families sit in the bellies
which appear and disappear,
idle and active,
waiting or surging
in wakes across the water

Festooned with washing
and a necklace of tyres,
these dowagers of the east
are enveloped
in diesel and cooking
diluted by each whiff of wind.

As generous as poets
who share their lines,
as composed as old ladies
who shuffle the jetty,
the junks' deportment
displays a wisdom of the past
with no need
for a superhighway in the present.

Stress

Is in the heat
of the breathless street,
in beggars' outstretched plastic cups,
in struggles for a new world order
through the old violence
or in the anonymity of women poets
in the sixteenth century

and in my tightening
as if the man approaching on the dark street
wants revenge for the pains of esteem
and I am the next victim.

Looking ahead I pretend
this is not my world.
He passes
and when the pause time comes
I recall occasions
of stray words which hurt
and led to stifling silence
or the lows of isolation rescued
by the sight of airmail etching
'I am here, I have written',

at which point I imagine
calm and elation
on a summer evening after Grapelli
followed by a long night sleep,
waking
without a hint of stress.

Punctuation

Endings can signal
the pointlessness
of journeys into a void
of no touching
and no confirmation through recognition
in travels to a new location
where the blank slate starts again,

a good reason for disliking full stops.

Whereas the promise of commencing
the same trip with familiar companions
offers communication
which needs no rehearsal
or humour that need not be explained,
in tandem with feelings
that shades of the seasons
are always escorted
by the certainty of their coming,

as in threads announced by semicolons.

In encounters with show-off scenes
humility is a nugget
to be fondled
when all around
is pomp, publication
and drama over inconsequentials,

as trumpeted by exclamation marks.

Blot on Jervis Bay

A yellow and turquoise refuge
whispers to searchers for sunshine and suntans
that even the gum trees
are grateful for the windless warmth
which nothing may disturb,

Disappointment comes suddenly
from an orange and black cowboy
squeezing libido from his bucking bronco,
storming the silence, throttling the waves
and, like oil on new snow,
wounding the body of the day.

Thanks to Degas

A summer's day lilt
covered by leaves
of light white cottons
or delicate silks
resembles the fruit
which inspired Degas
to be so generous with his feelings
as to share them with posterity
in stretched out lines
of back and buttocks
festooned by the languid look
and falling hair
of his completed nude.

Exploring Injustice

Bail Hearing

Splashing with an eye
to watching mothers,
children pretend to swim.

Pin-striped and bespectacled,
bulging on his bench,
the judge shows his hand
about the charges
against the innocent-until-otherwise
gaunt and long-haired defendant.

A reference to drugs
is a cue for licence
to quote from police tapes
to confuse the guilty issue
with the decision
whether the prisoner can be trusted
to arrive on time
for the serious business to follow.

The justice asks smart questions,
'is the drug's chemical base
something I would put in my pool?'

I can see him in his pool
floating belly-up, buoyant
that he has acquired the right things
by doing the right things
and the world will view him
a successful and just performer.

The world is a fool.
To an audience
who know they cannot throw things,
the rotund of the centre stage
mouths and licks his morals
in legal monotones
then delivers his denial.

Lifestyles are on trial
tho' the trappings of law
and practised politeness
give an appearance
of something being seen to be done.

The children also go through the motions
but even the proudest mothers know
their little ones are not really swimming.

The American Left In Conference

Moustaches drooping,
                 policies fomenting
Grey hairs crinkled
                 children in creches
Inevitable beards
                 familiar clichés
Moonlike spectacles
                 with rainbow visions
Non-violent language
                 for infinite justice
Friendships assumed
                 in bear-like hugs
Breasts swinging breezily
                 papers bundled in beige
Flapping shirt tails
                 controlled debates
Ample bums
            intense shoulders
                      slack jeans
                         and hopeful ideology

The Australian Right in Conference

Red velvet drapes
                carpets and palms
Identikit suits
                perfumed manners
Greying temples
                starched white shirts
Few women
                lots of graphs
In virgin plastic
                clean-shaven papers
Ordered visions
                cluttered theories
Economic blues
                by unemployed blacks
Irrational lovers
                unwanted babies
Down with taxes
                up with charity
Subsidies never
                independence for ever
Wobbly judgements
                precisely tailored
                        self-assured
                              and morally absurd.

Thirty Years Ago

In dark November I learned
from a radio
beaming to a free Europe
a name, Nagy,
in a revolution by a river
and I wondered about students and workers
being crushed
in tandem with my naivety.

We wondered how to protest
for those without graves
who are not to be remembered
but there is a place
where poppies bloom in the hay
and cover the young men who might have been.

The Pest Lorinc cemetery
is obscured by non-existent poems,
plays, movies and memorials
from mothers who survived
their executed sons.

Saying no to bitterness
is our tribute
to Jozsef, Lajos, Janos or Gyorgy,
whose faces would be inspiring to see
in the drizzle of this darkness
shepherded by a street lamp
that lights recollections
of condolences unspoken
for those revolutionaries
of thirty years ago.

Gun Control Rally

The ten thousand leaflet day
of automatics crossed with olives
begins with a gutsy, singing
of the frightened and of spouses
who loved till they blew their brains out.
She is applauded by supporters armed
with make-believes and the slogan
'we need guns like a hole in the head.'

Speakers sound ballistics –
seven hundred per year, fourteen per week,
more slain at home than in Vietnam.

Across the lawns
amplifications boom spectres
of men who might have been mad,
or jilted, or too tired to realise
their unrepeatable solutions.

The banners flap
towards those who stayed away.
More elusive than mass murderers,
they leave the protesters with little to aim at
save thoughts that the disinterested
may resurrect the fifties boredom
with an eighties blindness
to the issues of their dangerous age.

Privatisation

Prospectus

Deregulation has too many syllables
to sound artistic
yet this catch-your-breath prescription
for financial fornication
is dangled like a lexicon
with the décor of incentives and rewards
for users paying
for their own cost benefit equation.

The message is elevated
to a royal tour brass sound
with instructions to deposit
with striped merchants whose empathy
is akin to accountants' appeals
for charges which are not fees
but might be taxes
wrapped in the illusion
of a net transfer of your interest.

Thank you. Understanding is knowing
that taxes are high even if low
and a decrease in students receiving assistance
can be called profit
if uneven distribution means equality
and the ultimate Houdini knot
is a miracle cure of the product
which keeps the disease going,
like smoking your way to health.

Investments

Our balance of trade deficit
and investors' lack of confidence
is caused by an increase in poor widows
so we need an aphrodisiac
for the impotence of the over-fifty-million class
like a golden ticket
to the chocolate wonka bars
of the paper factory
where you could make your contribution
to overseas loans
for black holes in BMW suburbs.

Forget the distant old man
'don't sell the family silver'

but keep your eyes on the rising curve
in global indicators clinking
before canvas and below Sotheby crystals
where the gilt of exchange
needs deals of compliance
from bemused viewers
roofless or workless
yet asked to be accountable and pay
for hospital kleenex or timed local calls.

Dividends

With fewer syllables
efficiency looks easier
and could eliminate the unprofitable
by avoiding the safety measures
which used to keep airlines from crashing
in harmony
with those speaking-in-tongues dealers
flexing their free masonry support
for only some children's learning.

In place of a national poetry
prosaic recipes,
the sell-it-all hallucinogens
delivered through the decade's simple medicine,
the mind-bending basics:
give us your brains
and we'll deliver your thoughts,
worship the market like the media
groping for ratings
eyeing the production
of a bit of shampoo for the few
and endless soap for the many.

The Jury's Return

On this day of the jury's return
nordic islands
signpost the speedboats' trails,
the gulf stream has released
the secrets of winter
and twelve commoners
have ignored their instructions

which were blind to these beaches
and the thin soil
spotted by midsummer night's bells
and a gallery of gulls
applauding the mackerel

while in the distant court
humanity also celebrates
and the two defendants
have taken off the judge's clothes.

(Refers to the acquittal in June 1991 of Michael Randle & Pat Pottle
by an Old Bailey jury on a charge of conspiring to help the master
spy George Blake escape from prison)

Bomb Scare

Midmorning faces
in no-eye-contact silence
are receiving reassurance,

'we apologise for the inconvenience,
leave no luggage
and report any left'
which is not affecting snorers,
earphoned listeners and smothering lovers
oblivious to the prospect of aggression.

'As soon as we know
we shall let you know'
comes the rising calm
of Caribbean cockney
guarding London's highs and lows

who are common in compliance
and reading 'fight for life' headlines
about yesterday's explosion,
'pass right down the carriage please
we apologise for the inconvenience.'

Failing the Draft

I was watching the Vietnamese body count
when a summons invited me
to be interviewed for a uniform.

My sudden pulse rate confirmed
I would not be calm under fire.
I pretended indifference
– look them in the eye stuff –
and tossed it with bravado
into a wastepaper basket,

then sweated for three weeks
until it came again, with a red repeat
'attend for examination'.
The bravado gave way
to strategies for failing:
the wrong hair style or a confession
to liking pacifist articles
in tourist magazines
and a recall of allergies
about enemies in faraway places.

Without influential parents
the draft board would not be delayed.
When the day came they called my name,
a doctor said, 'remove your shirt,
drop your trousers, breathe deeply, cough.'
I was exhausted from last night's nightmare
– in which I drew a low lottery number –
my mottled neck was camouflage
and the mole on my cheek looked
like a push button for a missile.

The elderly doctor seemed deafened
by my palpitations. Sombre, he asked,
'do you have a history of hypertension?'
which made my non-soldier heart
thunder on. I told him today's performance
was normal. He wanted to be comforting.
'At your age,' he said, 'you should get this seen to.
This may be disappointing,
it seems you will not be fit enough
to fight for your country.'

Peace Class

Learning the names
of other students
is a handrail for probing
the violence of the invisible
or the Mahatma mysteries
of the satyagraha
salve for today's conflicts

which could be healed
by the language of dance,
tension release in role plays
or those assured mornings
of music and poetry
which harmed no one.

May your biographies
– more than a story
of secret competition for grades –
be a picture that sustains
struggles to unmask
the meaning of peace.

Free Trade

In multinationals' interests
a game is finalised
by insiders' rules
applauded by savants
whose creed this has always been.

I am an African father
pleading for work in a country
choked by two crops only conditions
for the repayment of debts
sold by talk of level playing fields.

I am an Asian mother,
my possessions swamped
by the world's rivers,
my children dying
in free trade zones.

I am your average newspaper reader
with acronym confusion
the GATT and NAFTA deals
for hamburger chains
to obliterate old skills and tastes.

We are Mr & Mrs modest mortgage
blinded by balance sheets,
mystified by growth
prescribed for our interests
by only a few players.

Peace Conference

Promised a dialogue to show
security for all to know
an ignorance of poverty
with global right to dignity.

Yet chemistry of noisy men
stopped chance of hearing once again,
so many modest Asian views
remain unheard and still are news

to those who always have dropped names
in rational academic games
to bolster status and the west
by humbly saying they know best.

So silent views we did not seek
but stared and turned the other cheek
while peace was caught in double bind
locked in the silos of their mind .

Lunch By the Picket Line

All month the wharfies have been locked out
by uniforms with dark dogs
and bullies with their bulletins
that prosperity depends on efficiency
when corporations achieve more
by workers making do with less.

Over a tuna sandwich
we eat the week's post-mortems
before sauntering
past 'MUA here to stay'
and 'outlaw the scabs'
signs directed at hooded men with rottweilers.

The harbour air
has Waltzing Matilda optimism
sung by players pondering a next move
towards police keeping them out
when the High Court
ruled they could go in.

Yesterday's protesters
have become today's street-side picnic
of talkers and dreamers and men knowing
here is a shackle for the next century
unless broken by ferrymen and firemen,
nurses and teachers, miners and sailors
in one-voice unison
which this lunch hour shows
temporarily over the tuna
permanently in recognition
that picket line solidarity
may be seldom seen or sensed
in the outward satisfaction
of comfort in the suburbs.

Visa Application

Never again will I judge
computers to be intrusive
compared to the inscrutables
who are recording dates of birth
and times of expected departure
for the recent arrivals
from flight TG 946.

Different nationalities
receive their dose of regulations.
No jokes crack the silence
as everyone seems mindful
that the twenty-dollar charge
and one hour of waiting
is a small price to pay
towards the recovery of a country
which even photographed the four years
of its own mutilation.

Explaining Genocide

I keep going up dead ends
as numbing as potholes
which lead to the killing fields,
as frustrating as the latest
official instruction,
'it would be better to forget'.

Which sounds like a diversion
for perpetrators
who have disappeared into the wet season
and feels like another slap
for survivors
who are also victims

lost in the shrouds of ghosts
in a culture's reluctance to reflect
that an executioner's gentleness
when he comes home
conceals the torture
in his hours at work.

The answer lies in knowing
that sadism lurks beyond shadows,
cruelty is fed by simplicity
and there can be no explanation
save in the obligation
never to cease to ask 'why?'

Kosovo from a Bangkok Restaurant

Children are the same the world over,
they don't really know
what is going on,
they love picking their noses
and gazing at the results.

Yehudi Menuhin must have known
what would be going on.
He has managed to die
just before Europe
began to conceive another catastrophe.

'First Ferry' Rules

Smoking and gambling
are not permitted on the voyage.
Disobedience will be
faced with persecution.
Thank you for your cooperation.
We wish you an enjoyable journey.

First-class Inequality

Years ago I felt ashamed
about the introduction
of fees for undergraduate students
and voted against.

Now I hear again the proposition
that encouraging inequality
is the way to become first class.

I am not in a position to vote now
but at least we ought to discuss this.

Devastation in Dili

A gentle sea is close yet far away,
a few palms bend to say there was a past
when shops and homes were sites of love's exchange
but now the city has been fired and crushed
by hatred and a lusting for revenge
against the votes of independence day.

Street after street, there are no signs of lives
when conversations lived between these walls
whose blue graffiti like a spider crept
where kerbs have crumbled and the trees are stumps
sticking like amputated limbs, as though
nothing loyal to Timor could be kept.

Charred beams support no roofs where iron rusts
in shapes of death and poverty lies wrapped
amid the crap of waste whose silent men
have disappeared to borders as a wind
with justice not in sight, only a mime
as though this rape was pleasure not a crime.

United Nations Presence

Reassurance from their
blue and white signs
is dulled by rows
of stationary four-wheel drives.

Mission clarity is cluttered
by the career paths
of multilingual feeders
of this latest bureaucracy.

Insecurity among
those they have come to save
is barely touched
by large boots
in a many nations mosaic
which departs and returns
to the security of the compounds.

Did You See *Four Corners*?

Capable of being a nation's once-a-week conscience
at least for those who watch,
but tonight's display of detention
for those who would be free
has had people saying
'we want 'mateship', 'fair go', 'she'll be right'
and 'down with tall poppies'
claims about our identity... revised
to show a taste for razor wire
to keep out asylum-seekers
to protect our democracy,
as explained by the holier-than-thou
who dehumanises
so that people escaping murder
will count their chances and decide
that in addition to sharks, crocodiles and deserts
everyone will be as inhospitable as him,
so it's not worth coming
even in this direction
especially as our penal past has reawakened
a love of locking up
far away from public view
yet on this occasion a smuggled camera
has allowed the interested to see,
the desperate a chance to plead
and by this *Four Corners* expose
has revealed a minister's cruelty
barely disguised by his pomposity.

Wide Country Refuge

A wide brown country
of skylines of homesteads
dotted with forests
which hinder the threat
of being strangled by salt

drinks from scalloped dams
to nurture a patchwork
of hopes and crops,

which are already a solace from cities
and could become a refuge
for all the world's refugees.

The World May Never Be the Same Again

New York pictures show the dust of death
and firemen digging to avoid despair
described in mourning through a million words,
the world may never be the same again.

Yet beeches burnished by an autumn wind
elsewhere are changing as they always did
and flintstone walls erect round stately homes
still stand as monuments to ancient crafts,

while on Broadhalfpenny Down the cricketers
in flannelled white play for unbroken time
and horses grazing in the dipping sun
are munching silhouettes for everyone.

Back on the other side the rubble mounds
are called ground zero where the divers dived
followed by thousands as the twin towers crushed
victims without a hope and most not found
even as bits of life's impermanence.

Unless we see the horses in the fields
or marvel at the skills which built those walls
and count the lovers' candles for the loved
to dull the hates, divert the schemes for wars,
the world may never be the same again.

Ruddock's Rules

A contemporary drama of mateship, compassion, understanding fair play and generosity in fourteen verses. The only scene a nightly media monologue from the Minister for Punishment and Repatriation.

'I am cold and grim, of unsmiling face
but I really love the human race
and tho' I punish those I can,
I'm a liberal, reasonable Christian man.

I'm not sadistic but I do deplore
the rules of international law
and why do people make a fuss
of over-stayers who look like us ?

The facts are there, the story goes,
just watch this nightly TV pose,
I never smile, I'm full of reason,
especially in the smuggling season

when a Middle Eastern swarthy horde
have thrown their children overboard,
which may not be true but why the fuss,
these people have shown, they're not like us.

They queue with gold from Iraq to Iran
to meet a reasonable Christian man,
they've heard of kindly Australian hosts
like sharks I describe around our coasts,

infested waters and dangerous cliffs
so I've clouded the world with Aussie myths:
humanitarian treatment for hire
in the forms of rolls of razor wire

placed for asylum-seekers' good
in Woomera and Villawood,
so come here to stay with your children too
we're generous people we welcome you,

we take too many but don't shed a tear
for the four thousand who came here just last year
from prison windows they can see the sand
and the empty space of our wide brown land.

My job is to fool those overseas
critics who encourage these refugees
I'm not inflexible, just watch my lips
sewn together with pollsters' tips

that Aussie voters all want to see
me posing as moral on TV
to free them from fear, to put them at ease
protected from strangers and new disease.

Now I've found a cure as simple as gravy,
show that we're macho, call out the navy.
To stop this smuggling, this prostitution
I've found it, I've got it, the Pacific Solution.

Come to Nauru, I really can't wait
to show gulls' droppings becoming phosphate,
it costs a fortune, a small price to pay
to deter illegals by Aussie fair play

such as scorning the UN, giving it heaps
my Canberra allies, more bullies and creeps.
I must be unbending for the best game in town,
say 'no' to compassion and down with Bob Brown,
deride human rights, oh what a ripper
to scorn that Norwegian *Tampa* skipper.

Ignore our opponents, they're soft and they're fools
who can't read the small print of Ruddock's rules:
employ more guards, insist on retention
of penal traditions, control through detention,
deter, create fear, impose every ban
and pretend I'm a liberal, reasonable, Christian man.'

Exit to far right of rotting Australian political stage.

Tenth Anniversary of Mabo

In an unexpected dream
it is difficult to tell
whether dawn waters are shining
or – ten years on –
are an illusion from mists
when a few brave justices
recalled a record of the dispossessed
which history said had not happened
until with careful haste
they broke the mindset
of dire predictions
that losers would win and winners lose.

Over the red brown deserts
by picnic spots called tablelands,
across the soils of plenty
comes a prospect of lands restored
and health revived, as slowly
as self-respect can be sketched
in songlines smudged
when languages were lost
and the property men prevailed,
whose descendants now conclude
the Mabo mob should be grateful
for what might happen to day
and did not happen then.

Today a cormorant sits on the rocks.
No one challenges his poise or place
while in the courts they queue
for rock pools and riverbeds,
mostly for honouring, made possible
when miners started looking up
as well as looking down,
graziers readied for mediation,
lawyers tired of litigation
historians admitted the people were there,
the land was not empty,
a search for truth
has lulled the legacy of shame.

The Migrants' Welcome

They speak different languages
and arrived optimistic,
their achievements stamped by registrars
chancellors and untranslatable mottos
sealed in plastic
as pictures
of proud identity for new lives.

Soon these successes are labelled insufficient
by committees who 'tut tut'
to protect national standards
by discarding chunks of lives
and years of labour
from wherever these hopefuls
have travelled to the antipodes.

Letters of rejection
are lacquered with politeness
but the receivers have cried at their humiliation
via the adjudicators' ability
to persuade themselves
that they have acted
in everyone's interests.

We are left to wonder
why some cultures are called unworthy
amid self-congratulation
about non-discrimination
mixed with 'fair go's' for mateship
and hoorays for multiculturalism.

You have been welcomed
by being excluded.
You are appalled
and we are not even ashamed.

Cruelty

Lies not among the squawking of the gulls,
nor in the shifts beneath a surface calm
where dolphins dive and navigate the shoals
of whiting who are riding out a storm.

Lies not among the reptiles on the shore
or in large birds who soar without a song
gliding with eyes according to their lore
searching for those they think do not belong.

Was in Rwanda and the Gaza Strip,
in Ireland's terrors seen from either side
in codes which still sustain the stone and whip
or out of sight in Pol Pot genocide,

which felt the darkness of a Stalin purge
and then came Timor's hackers out to show
not even death deserved a funeral dirge,
they'd be as savage as in Kosovo.

But lies not here where human rights are prized
where leaders pose and want to make it clear
their words and actions show they're civilised
they love all children and have outlawed fear.

Yet take their views only from narrow shelves,
not moved by critics or by children's tears
they've drunk from Newspeak to delude themselves,
strict punishment removes the people's fears.

Thus speaks the minister who cannot miss
the target groups who like his liberal stand
each succoured by the talkback prejudice
denying haven in this wide brown land.

Anti-war Rally

The inspectors' search has ended dead,
a smoking gun cannot be found
some cities march each ill at ease
at spread of mad cowboy disease
while here one leader finds the groove
'democracy is on the move.'

The rhythm of an intent crowd
is oiled by sweat and reassured
by placards teaching as they sway
to reject what the pipelines say,
to lessen chance of people maimed
when lives are 'cost per gallon gained'.

While purple ribbons have proclaimed
a spirit of virility
which needs no gun from space or moon
but knows the insight from lampoon
for laughter disarms, combats fear,
see prime minister up a president's rear.

Warships in Jervis Bay

On manoeuvres
to practise searching for the unexpected,
yet out of place as tanks in a game park,
the grey and jagged silhouettes
prowl sluggish like predators.
From the shore there is no sign of life:
flotillas of steel and oil,
of electronics, blood and weapons
ply their trade where dolphins play.

Where waves fall on stranded seaweed
the only signs of death
are cast-up cuttlefish, bluebottles
and – marooned in the sand –
the arm of a tree trunk
rinsed by the retreating wash,
immersed by the incoming swell,
a headstone for an end to life
or a lens of lessons
for invisibles steering the sea.

The stout wood could have been
the masthead of a ferry, a schooner's boom
or a trader's plank. It is now my frame
for peering at destroyers
and supply ships silent yet proclaiming
this ocean is ours to limber up
for a faraway bombing
to guard democracies,
to guarantee security.

The sailors could learn
from shoals pursued by gulls,
or a bald eagle swooping
apparently wise
and everyday contemplating,
with neither paint nor rigging,
without guns, radar or a compass
when to glide and when to dive
for succour from the waters,
to maintain balance in the bay.

Crossing to Ramallah

The embassy advised 'don't go',
my friend said 'get a diplomatic pass',
an Israeli peacemaker said
'don't look like an American',
the *Jerusalem Post* described the kidnap of a taxi driver,
Haaretz reported a Palestinian researcher mobbed
for concluding that refugees were not interested
in the right to return.

My blood pressure is burbling like a nation in waiting,
my tank for composure is running on empty,
akin – when I was eight –
to jumping from a high board
but I was a coward then
and the question is
whether I am any different now?

As protection against the risk of mistaken identity
I have chosen cream trousers and a navy blue shirt.
I'll be carrying a green folder
and a copy of my host's book,
my proposed identikit picture
to hang somewhere between
a threat to one side's security
and a traitor to another's cause.

I am five foot ten, clean-shaven.
The unknown is faraway and close.
I wonder which taxi driver will agree to go,
whether the soldiers slept well
and are in a good mood,
if the driver sent to collect me
will recognize the book with the green folder
and my cream-trouser presentation of normality.

Occupied Territories

Walls rise in the mind's eye
and are difficult to climb.

Liberty lies within curfews
but contains no right to be free.

Crying is unwise
because nothing will absorb the tears.

Humour lies infertile
unless brutality is the court jester.

Refugees are preparing their journey
but towards a mirage.

Humiliation is a daily diet
which nurtures no one.

Domination is a customary stance
which gains no pride

in a land where the sun
creates neither shadows nor shelter,
burns the veiled and the bare-headed
and is still lighting the fuses of history
in conformity with rituals
which have guaranteed only
an identity for the dead.

Disappointing Sunday Papers

High on expectations
of excavating nuggets
to cut and paste at the weekend
I am dismal from repetition
of yesterday's atrocities
minus questions about the fuse which lit them,
dulled by accounts of corporate swindlers
and of footballers sin-binned for their muscles,

yet my worst frustration
– like a prospector's vain sifting –
is a columnist's attempt to be funny
by announcing his satire toward a punchline
which arrives blurred
and leaves me
as listless as this page turning is fruitless,
as expressive as sighs of optimism lost
because I had looked forward to the digging,
had set time aside
and had expected so much.

Composition of Destruction

From Berlin to Birmingham,
New York to Copenhagen,
the physicists examined
the darkness of their contradictions.
In harmony and in collision
they journeyed where thinking hurt
and a faithful third party realised
that the dancing of easier times
forecast the dangers of the present.

The music in their aspirations
saw understanding
as a prize for equations
showing matter as waves
in the freedom of a chain reaction
which also proclaimed
the bass clef of a Manhattan Project,
that 1940s IVF unit
to hasten the birth of a bomb.

The notes of their thoughts
became the verbs of their conversations
about quantum as the smallest coin
for bargaining and trading
the isolation of an isotope,
yet neither friend nor enemy could be certain
whether the orchestra they were assembling
would sound a new dawn
or a last night.

Descriptions of probable destruction
required a poet's licence
of words to contain energy,
from fusion and fission of natural uranium
to particles as photons
and barium under bombardment,
a display of the real as fiction
as trust between Bohr and Heisenberg
was eroded by the silence of suspicion.

These were scientists not musicians,
mathematicians not poets,
inventors protecting their patents
in times torn by the deportation of Jews,
and by an occupation whose ending
suggested a striving toward Hiroshima
calculated from complements
whose only guarantee
was the principle of uncertainty.

(A composition born from Michael Frayn's play *Copenhagen*)

Tell Me the Truth About War

A coalition of the willing declared war
but did not explain why,
or the reasons they gave
were not the real reasons
and something called a dodgy dossier
became as smelly as the exam papers
of a schoolboy who cheated.

One leader is an evangelist,
another a true believer,
each hooked on the catechisms of their convictions
and would be lost without reference to their Gods
though non-believers
have questioned the sacred texts
and have asked for evidence.

An evil man was supposed
to be able to destroy his opponents
with mighty weapons in forty-five minutes
but the leaders who wanted to eliminate a dictator
also needed to throw their weight around,
use their weapons
to convince the world of their truth:
by killing people to protect them
they would be welcomed in the streets,
by installing puppet governments
their armies could demonstrate democracy at work,
which was another good reason for having a war.

Fantastic News

In the half light of the half heard
politicians are apologising for violence,
and when told that weapons are a sign of weakness
men in uniform are undressing,
extremists have been diagnosed
with stomach cramps caused by dogmatism
and the spring-water frankness of the next sound bite
refers to blown off limbs of dark-eyed children
being the achievement of cluster bombs
and troops dead from friendly fire
have woken to say that in future
they would prefer to face their enemy,

at which point I rub my eyes
and increase the volume:
missiles are still the figures of speech,
a highly trained baboon with slick hair
and bombed-out syntax
is explaining that freedom
means contracts for partners to rebuild,
that looting the past is an untidy part of war,
limited casualties 'on our side'
can be counted a victory,
water will be restored
and we should all be grateful.

Revolution of Conscience

As tho' whiplash could be controlled,
he wrestled revenge
with a prophet's concern for justice.
From lunch counters, buses and pulpits
his vision gave strength
to those who had expected so little.

His love, never anaemic,
was a courage for equality
detailed in street marches
for bus riders and garbage collectors
and in a dream
which became everyone's music.

Optimism born from non-violence
in a revolution against slavery
acknowledged the Mahatma's dictums
that everybody is somebody,
a treasure not easily found
on the continents of a new century
which yearns for lessons of liberation
from the conscience of Martin Luther King.

Non-violence of Surfers

Watching horizons for the swell,
riding the lifting, subsiding
into the equanimity of their vocation
they are confident in their knowing
and do not need to be assertive.
On a sun-drenched surface
three surfers wait on their boards,
savouring togetherness
by being alone with the sea.

Like the momentum for justice
which will surely come,
an increase in the swell
is a warning for the starter's call
to point shorewards,
their energy focused on the flow,
a paddlewheel of feet and hands
reaching top-gear frenzy on the crest

and on this wistful morning
they are off in the truth of their freedom
found in the happiness of a generous wave.

'Be Thankful for Small Mercies'

Is a cliché for responding
to complaints over the cost of living,
the late arrival of electricians or plumbers,
the untidiness of children,
the unfaithfulness of husbands
or even the failure of relations to say 'thank you'
for carefully chosen Christmas presents.

Logic demands that comparing oranges to lemons
– joy on the birth of an all things intact baby
compared to news of the less than perfect arrival –
may be like arguing from another planet,
akin to a promotion for deafness
in response to a president's plans
for a space station on Mars.

When life's rivers flow unhindered
– switches always give light
water washes every skin,
shelves fill the trolleys –
dams need to be witnessed and losses weighed:
a neighbour's hair-losing nausea-causing treatment,
the nobody-loves-me droop of the proud mother
who once paraded her successful partner,
let alone the UN's latest infant mortality figures
or the US military's admission
of thousands of innocents dying
because they have been liberated.

The best caution against complaining
would be to see asylum-seekers' lips
sewn in response to the agony
of being so inconsequential
as to be considered unworthy of any mercies
save the prospect of being returned
to the places they wanted to leave

and for this reluctant recognition
they have now ensured
they will be unable
even to say 'thank you' for that.

It's been a bad week for spies

Making a profession of deceit
has received an establishment rebuke
for showing that intelligence decorators
had spewed oils on a canvas
needed by war's enthusiasts
who were grateful for the picture
but had overlooked the needs of people
who were asked to believe
that in the search for threats and enemies
the spooks were for them,
their evidence could be counted
and that a habit of saying something different
from what you knew
would not be considered clever.

Recipes for false marriages
of MI5 to MI6 to the FBI & CIA
to be joined at the hip
to their offspring ASIOs and ONAs
is reported
to have produced suspicion about cooperation
when egos demanded a competition
to find the most sensational eavesdropper
judged by the most improbable story
likely to be labelled
a breakthrough in defence.

At least dismay can be expressed
at the outstretched hands of beggars
but like a gasp in response to being mugged
only disbelief seems possible
at the games
of those who used to be contained
within a John le Carré novel
yet are now so numerous
that they have ended up on our doorsteps,
not to know us
but to experiment with their listening devices.

The life-enhancing properties of spying
are as difficult to swallow
as advertisements for workshops
where creamed hair in sharp suits
promise a weekend of learning to make a million,
yet the people's trust in intelligence
is a leap of faith into corridors
where watching and listening
are as dangerous as unprotected sex,
where a pandemic of the faceless
are creating secrets
when Bangladesh is under water
and the latest official reports
say the spies have not been very clever
even at interpreting their software
through the prism of their dark glasses.